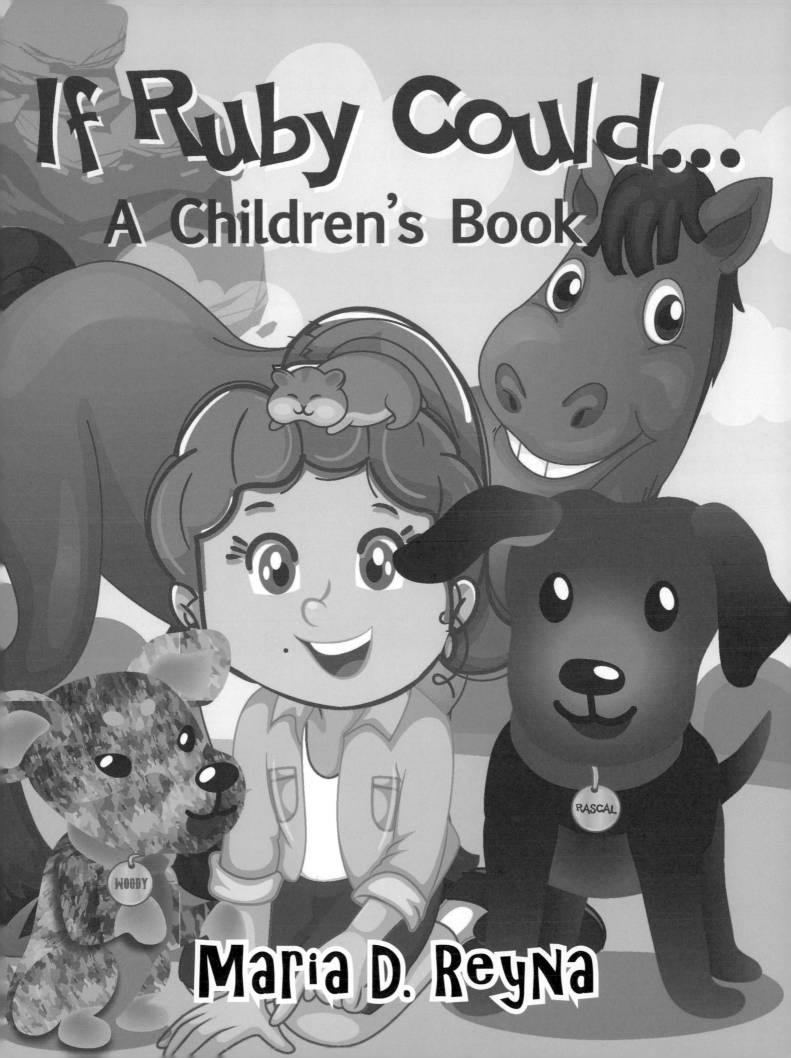

iUniverse books may be ordered through booksellers or by contacting:

iUniverse
1663 Liberty Drive
Bloomington, IN 47403
www.iuniverse.com
844-349-9409

ISBN: 978-1-6632-2762-1 (sc)
ISBN: 978-1-6632-2761-4 (e)

Library of Congress Control Number: 2021916415

Print information available on the last page.

iUniverse rev. date: 08/27/2021

To Ruby

You colored my world...
the walls, the tables, the chairs.

Ver. 1.0
07/29/2020
If Ruby Could
A Children's Book
Maria D. Reyna

If Ruby could take home
the homeless animals
she encounters on a
regular basis, she would.

Ruby is five years old and
wants to be a veterinarian
when she grows up.

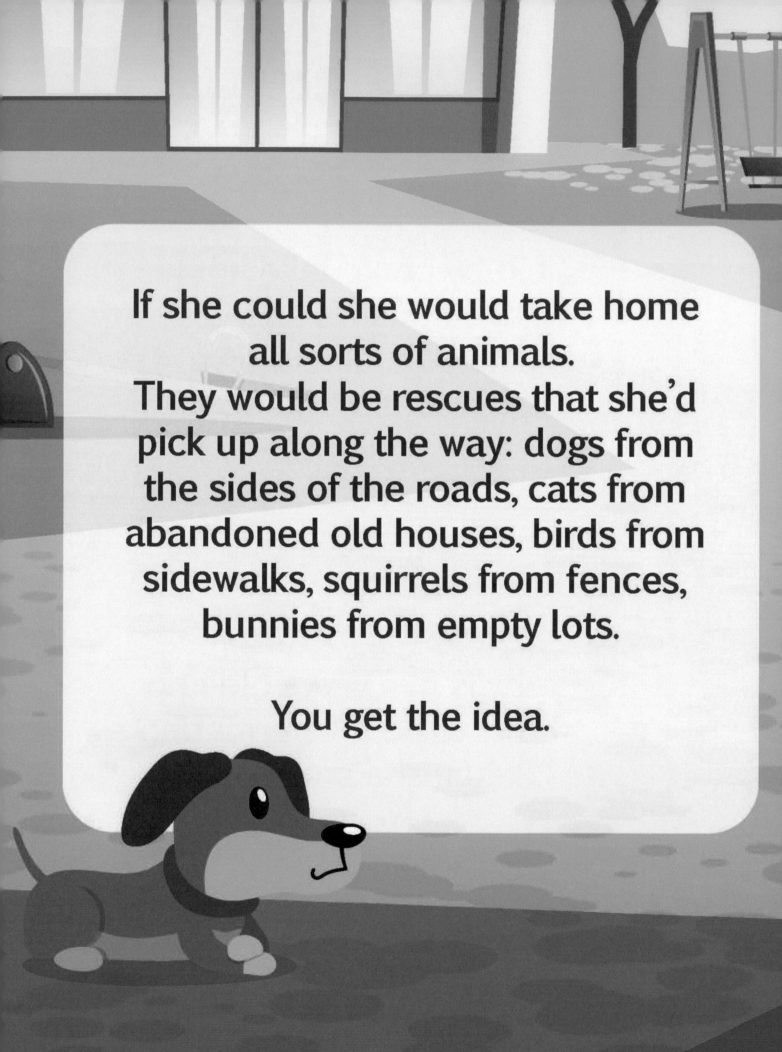

If she could she would take home
all sorts of animals.
They would be rescues that she'd
pick up along the way: dogs from
the sides of the roads, cats from
abandoned old houses, birds from
sidewalks, squirrels from fences,
bunnies from empty lots.

You get the idea.

She would make sure to keep them clean. Teeth brushed, manes brushed, tails fluffed. She would need some help tending to them. For this she would need her own dog, Woody.

He would keep them from straying off, and would play with them so they had a fun day.

The Horsie

Ruby's horse would like carrots and apples along with his regular food. He would love to run and jump. He would especially like to lay in the shade while she sat beside him and read to him.

Her horse's name would be Chocolate. She would walk him and pet him. She would comb his long mane and give him carrots.

Every day before going to bed she would make sure Chocolate was comfortable in his bed. Then she would kiss him good night.

The Doggies

Ruby's dogs would have their own kennels, except for Woody.   He is Ruby's buddy and sleeps in her room.   The dogs would have a kiddy pool to cool off in when it got hot, and plenty of blankets when it got cold.

Her dogs would love carrots and peanuts. Go figure. She would bathe them and brush them and clean their teeth. She would make sure they had clean breath. Her other dogs would be Rascal, Bosco, Rustaford (whom she called Rusty). Woody she named as such because of the colors of his fur.

The Kitties

Her cats' names would be Rodeo, Space Cadet and Furlo (words she heard on TV). They would have fluffy beds by the window and plenty of towels to dry off with after their baths. She would feed them tasty food that would keep them healthy.

She would also teach them how to play music.

The Bunnies

All her bunnies would be soft and cuddly. Confetti, Panson (Chubby) and Poodie would race in the grass and practice hopping. She would pet them and make sure their fur was squeaky clean. And she would teach them to skateboard.

The Turtlely

The turtle in Ruby's house would be a big and old turtle with a crack in its shell. Its name would be Goobies. She would feed it lettuce and apples, and would shine its shell and take it for walks every day.

The Hammies

The hamsters would be in a cage where they could climb up and down ladders, and take naps on their beds.   The Japanese hamster would be named DingDong, and the other one would be named Üsa.

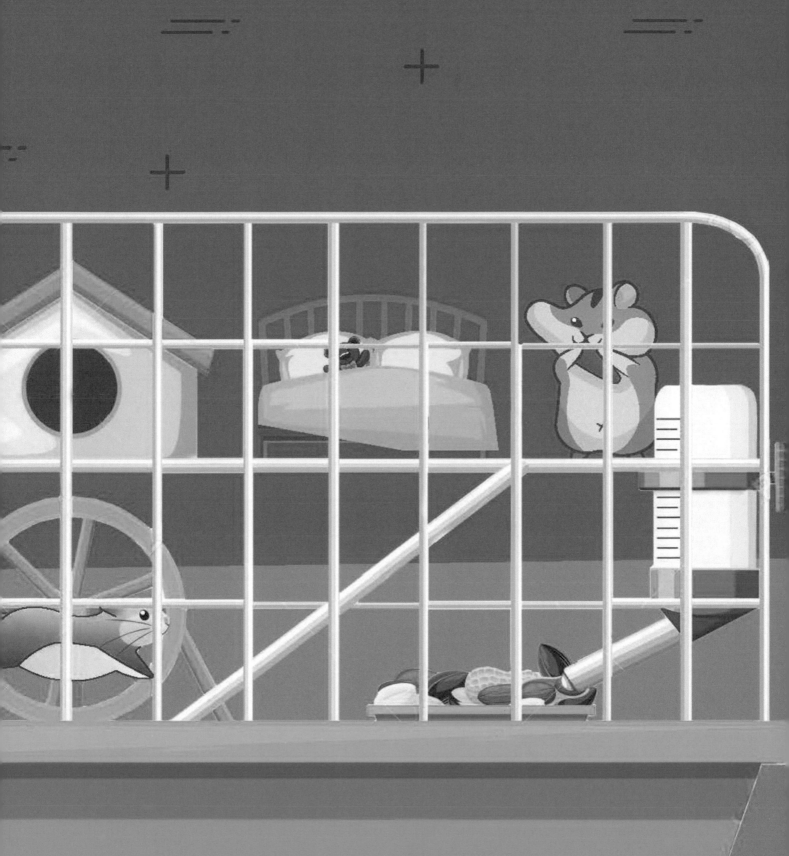

These are only some of the animals Ruby would have in her home, if mom would say okay.

Printed in the United States
by Baker & Taylor Publisher Services